The Moon
On
The Ruins

Acknowledgements

The author wishes to express his debt to those who helped in a material or inspirational way in making this work possible.

Preparation and Proof-Reading -
Sarah Brady
Bernadette Brady

Fr. Robbie McCabe

Cover: Carbury Castle, Co. Kildare

Published in Ireland by
Alesbury Books, Edenderry, Co. Offaly.
© Copyright - Philip Brady, 2001. All Rights Reserved.

Design and Typesetting - Artwerk, Dublin.
Printed and bound by ColourBooks Ltd, Baldoyle, Dublin 13.

A catalogue for this book is available from the British Library.
ISBN No. (cloth) 0-9525027-3-9
ISBN No. (paperback) 0-9525027-4-7

My first dreams were, and are, my best
I would rather take a free country walk,
leaving the roads for the less trodden paths of the hills
and the lanes,
than ride in a yacht or a coach;
I would rather see the moon in the ruins
than the gaslight of an assembly room;
what, in the name of everything we know,
would be to me the silver and gold of all Alaska!

W.H. Davies

From "The Autobiography of a Super-Tramp"

For
Patricia

Contents

Verse
&
Vignette

Revisiting

Assembled in time's overgrowth,
Resemblances that skipped a generation
To reappear in faces
Fresh from Croydon
To Alabama
To hear what once there was.

This is where the garden was,
Where cornflowers ran blue,
And roses twined their chromosomes
That hung and clung and hummed,
Where now a broad-leafed sycamore,
In sapling adolescence
Claimed their thorned crown.

The small stream ran here,
And gurgled through the stones
To pout and spout
Into the drinking well.
There was a music cascade here,
And typhus too,
With half whispered names
Of who succumbed,
In a world with no evil in it,
When the Great War had just begun.

The fields sloped down to Coles
Where wimpled swallows dived
Among gnats
Good weather high;
Each year they came
In counterfeited freedom,
By Moor's Alhambra and minaret call
To chapel bell and Gorman's shed:
They could see the likenesses
And the differences.

They had seen like faces here before,
Had seen a generation leave
Without reprieve,
To shouldered hod
Or collared God,
To Cedar Falls, Des Moines
To Portland, through the Rockies,
To Brisbane and to Banyo
Where among the gum trees
They heard the Kookaburras laughing,
Good shepherds bound to parables,
Or lambs led to their slaughter.

The loft was here,
For barn dance and spree.
It was here the seeds of Riverdance
Lay dormant on a dusty floor
Till brought to life
By flute and lilted reel,
And River-music too
Before its own Diaspora.
It was here
A Yankee girl one day
Came home and danced
The Highland Fling
With heels that afterwards
Grew longer into folklore,
When someone said
Her steps were "cogglesome"

The fort was down the lane
Where it had turned
Away in fear,
And would not trespass,
And after dark they said
That someone strayed around
Inside, till daybreak.
The foxglove unchecked thrived
Till plucked today for prayer
To serve our altar of remembrance.

The tart taste on the billberry
Awoke adventures still,
And nearer home
The sheugh was overgrown,
Where on a blackened knapweed head
The *tortoiseshells* would weigh
And wait,
And flit among the thistles
Where opened *peacock* eyes,
Ferocious in deceit
With *common white*
Traced patterns in their flight
Of delicate infinity.
The cows delayed here
Stall bound
For chains grown silver
With submission,
And cackling geese were stilled.

That field there, forninst us,
Was where the tubers grew.
The early Epicures in bloom
With bluestone rims
Against the blight,
And Aran Banners bulked
For feeding troughs.
Later still
The dark skinned Aran Victor
Purple on the ridge was picked
Till famished hands grew numb.

On a haw day in November,
When the frost had crossed the sun
The Brent geese
On an Arctic feeding string,
Free as a kite, bound to the wind
Called out above potato pits,
Where rush and clay
Kept school fees stored,
For twice a year
A litter fed
Would go to market.

The window there,
Half boarded,
Is where the cards were played.
The five, the knave, the ace of hearts;
And to renege,
The unforgiven sin of broken trust.
'Twas here they haeved the trump
Or led the drait,
And with the embers low
They finished with the game
They called the scuaibín,
And if they did not gain life's wealth
They had its riches.

This was where the haggard was,
Where stacks were threshed and winnowed
Till axles deep in chaff
Grew muffled,
And straw reeks grew and billowed
For bed and thatch and fodder,
And oats that spilled were bagged
And milled for skillets
And a breakfast table.

In that room there
Each child was born,
A parent, and a grandparent;
The settle bed,
The stable lamp,
The midwife's jug
And tinsmith's basin.
They took what came
By ebb and flow,
The moon looked down in silence;
They bore their loss
And reared their gain,
And thanked their God for hardships.

We left behind a citadel,
A fortress filled with values
And "God willed" tribulations,
Deep rooted in the Drumlins:
It drew us back
And watched us disappear again
To terraced gardens
And petunia pots,
To hybrid city borders
Of agapanthus
And begonias growing rootless
In their hanging baskets
Of Babylon.

The American

I met a man
By the canal bank once,
Out at the Lock in Ticknevin.
He wore his great coat in July,
His only coat,
His Gospel coat;
The same for winter snow,
For he had no other.

"You're from New York"!
To a stranger there, he said,
"Your first time here!
My mother's brother went there long ago,
Another to Montana.
When it's quiet here," he said
"You can hear the birds singing.
You'd think you were in heaven."
He had a single tooth
Of dubious use;
He watched the waters move reflectively,
And said *"It's Heaven."*

Had their parents traded places long ago,
When some were forced to go,
He would have a wardrobe now,
A signet ring,
For education;
But where the young swans glide
He would not know
The birds singing.

The Bluebells

The bluebells have gone
From the mountains
Where they stood
Once azure on the slope,
In their tiers of deep blue
Among ferns
In the springtime
And summer of hope.

The bluebells still sing
To the river
That tumbles in streams
Over stones,
To the runes
Of an ice-age retreating
That clings
To the pathways it hones.

The bluebells come back
To the mountains,
As sure and azure
As of old.
Do they come back
Without an emotion
To watch dreams they once gave us
Growing old?

Forgotten Photograph

Black and white, boxcamera'd,
Teenaged hopes
Arched on a doorstep,
Programmed for happiness,
Where parents seemed old
In a world still young
To be moulded, changed
And fitted to our dreams.

How did we succeed,
We, who have taken our parents' places
As our teenage children
Have now taken ours?
We listened to their music -
"The Spinning Wheel",
Threads flowing backwards
From a child's piano,
"When you and I were young, Maggie"
And forwards
From that old black and white snapshot.

We would not know,
Could not know
The toil, the fears
The unshed tears,
The aches of hope jettisoned,
Replaced by what was real.
Maybe we did better
Than our dreams;
Maybe!

"The Spinning Wheel"
Would weave a magic,
Each child would spin,
Would bloom, would fade,
Move on.

Could we ever be as sage
As those parents once were;
Could we ever have been
As guileless
As these children now are;
For, once
We threw our arms around the world,
Omniscient,
And still
Our minds have not grown old.

Who has guided us
Through those changing minefields
Of ideals?
Who has saved us
From our dreams?
Maybe we have done better
Than our dreams
Through those changes thrust upon us.

Hundreds come and go
And say hello,
A friend awhile through circumstance.
A handful will remain
That will not change with fashion,
Where time is not a matter.
What do you say
When after thirty years
A stranger says
"You have not changed"

You know you are the same,
A photo-frame away,
Arranged by chance one day;
The world is young
And time is not a matter.

The Woman and the Choir

Lord grant us the gift of your peace:
Peace in our hearts; Our homes; Our world.
Make us the instruments of your peace.
Fr. Michael beckoned peremptorily.

I was crossing the square, in front of the Basilica, and starting the short ascent to St. Joseph's Gate, which leads out to the hotels and the shops of Lourdes.

Would I read a prayer at the International Mass in the underground tomorrow morning? It had been several years since I attended that mass. My last recollection of this event was of its vastness, its diverse languages, its confusing universality, its crowds pushing and pulling, trying to find space where none existed in the world's biggest Basilica.

"Yes", I said, *"It would be a privilege".*

It was as well to be positive when it was obvious that there was no escape.

"Be in the choir at 8.00 o'clock in the morning, sharp" he said *"and I will give you the reading".*

I was there early, before eight. The choir is a cordoned off area, opposite the altar, surrounded by a wooden rail. There were some singers already there - Dutch, German, Spanish, Irish and a scattering of other nationalities, all united in the common language of music. I nodded to someone I knew and took my seat. Others drifted into place. A priest from Ireland, acting as master of ceremonies glided towards us.

"Is there an English speaking reader here", he asked.

I answered by displaying my white piece of paper. A gesture and a finger pointed to the top corner inside the entrance gate. I took my place in the front row and waited.

The conductor arrived. Each singer took a book on entering. With a wave of his hands and a magic in his voice the practice began. The collection of individuals was suddenly transformed into a powerful and harmonious expression of beliefs and respect. For forty minutes the recital continued. The guest singer arrived. This was sheer magic, his voice pure music.

A few minutes before nine, the procession entered down the main aisle, with banners and colours of the nationalities involved. A man stood outside the choir gate with a camera to capture the scene, focusing on the choir. All around the space was thronged with wheelchairs in orderly rows. The man blocked a narrow passage as he paused holding up two others who were looking for a seat where none existed.

An old woman with a stick saw that her way was blocked. She reached across just as the camera's anti-red eye was flashing. She clipped him on the back of head, indicating with the stick that he was causing an obstruction and that he should move. She arrived at the choir gate. There was not a space anywhere. She leaned across the rails and looked straight into my corner,

"Can I get in there?", she said.

"This is only for the choir", I told her.

"Surely to God you wouldn't refuse a poor woman a chance to sit down", she said.

I tried to look away but her eyes were fixed on mine. I got up, went to the gate and slipped off the lock. In she came, stick, bags, the lot. I pointed across to the far side where there was some space still available. She looked over, surveyed the cosmopolitan scene -

"No" she said, *"they're all knobs. I'll sit down here beside you".*

There just wasn't space, so I took her by the elbow and as we started across, I heard a reprimand - cantors, cantors or something foreign to indicate that this was only for singers. But it was too late - the organ had started the entrance hymn - everyone was back to the singing. She made it to the second seat.

In the pauses between the music I saw her leave her stick on the floor. I held my breath as it clanged lightly. There were microphones everywhere, picking up the slightest sound. Next she reached into her plastic bag. I could hear every rustle as she rummaged and rummaged and to my horror out came another plastic bag. For the first time I began to pray - please don't let her take out sandwiches or a can of beverage. This would surely be picked up all around the auditorium when it popped and hissed and no one would know where it was coming from but me. This would make a terrific ad for a fizzy drink, as 20,000 heads turned, but please not today I prayed. To my relief it was not refreshments that emerged. She took out a small prayer book and beads. She sat quiet as a statue, frozen in thought, facing the altar. She positioned herself that, though seeing the altar, her peripheral vision, without moving her head, took in every movement of the choir.

I looked at my invocation.
Make us an *"instrument"* of your peace. Make us an *"instrument"* of your peace.
No it would be better say, Make *"us"* an instrument of your peace.

My big moment had arrived. The master of ceremonies had arrived back. He nodded to the first, the second, to me and one by one German, Dutch, English, Spanish, Italian lined up. There were about 20,000 present with closed circuit television for those with a poor view. We were all efficient and relieved that in our two lines of fame we did not let the side down. Back we came in procession.

We stood for the "Our Father". It was impressive. *And lead us not into temptation ——- and let us offer each other a sign of peace.* There were a few minutes of euphoria. Everyone was ecstatic and shook hands enthusiastically. Several left the choir and shook hands with the conductor. So did I, for I was in the front seat. Several shook hands with the guest singer because he was sensational. The old woman never moved and no one moved towards her. She kept her eye fixed on the altar and kept her beads clutched in her hand but in her peripheral vision she was acutely aware of the activity and the excitement around her.

After the last hymn there was a spontaneous and rapturous round of applause. There was enthusiastic congratulations all around. In the milling of the crowd the throng melted. I took a wheelchair to take someone back to the hospital. I looked around and the woman was gone.

It was about 11 o'clock that night when I was returning from the hospital. I walked back by the grotto as I usually do. At that hour of night it is one of the serenest places on earth in spite of the presence of people, a place of reflection. Out of the corner of my eye I saw someone I thought I knew, sitting alone. I looked again.

"Thanks for the sate" she said, in a broad Irish accent.

It was the old woman from the choir. She was holding two candles.

"I'm going to sit here all night" she said *"and I have two candles, one for the family and one for the dead".*

I sat down beside her and we talked.

"I couldn't come down last night because of the rain", she said, *"but I'll stay here all night. I'm seventy-seven and I've a broken home, one son is troubled in his mind and the other has brains and a BA but he is an atheist. So I'll sit here all night and pray. I know they didn't approve of me today"*, she said, *"but thanks for the sate".*

We parted company as good friends and I left her to her vigil.

I had only been back in the hotel a short while when another crisis arose. Someone who was very ill had deteriorated. I had to return to the hospital where I collected the emergency case. It was now 2.00 am and the entrance to the main square was long closed. The only access was by a walking route over the basilica and down through the trees. This is a narrow zigzag path, steep and tree lined, and is the only way open to the grotto after midnight. On my way back I became curious. Would my friend still be keeping her vigil? As I was passing the grotto I walked slowly around. I was disappointed. There were only five people there. She was not one of them. I really had not expected to see her and I headed again towards the zigzag path through the trees. Beyond the entrance to the path there are several candle shrines where candles burn all night. As I turned to go, a figure moved in the candlelight. I stalled and looked down through the flickering light.

"Glory be to God" came the voice. *"You couldn't be a doctor?"* said the woman emerging, and fixing her eyes on the black case.

"I was so ashamed today with this coat" she said *"but it was monsooning at home when I left, and it was all I had. I knew they were looking at me, but we bested them, me and you, didn't we"?* We both laughed heartily. I left by the zigzag path through the trees for the last time. The candlelight chased shadows across her face as I disappeared. She went back to her vigil, praying for impossibilities. I do not know if her prayers were answered or could be answered but as I started up the zigzag path for the last time I still could hear her laughing.

I thought, yes, there is some peace in her heart, her world, if only for one night and I chuckled to myself at the thought of how we had *"bested them"*.

White Martyrdom

He sat beneath the night sky
And watched the stars
Relentless in their path.
He knew when Sputnik due
Would weave unsteady path
Against his distant heavens.
He watched it climb
And dip across his firmament,
And closed his eyes
And thought he heard the ocean
Lap the warm sands
From Beira to Mombasa.

He flicked another bottle cap
And took a breath
Deep with the salt spray of far away.
A dik-dik
Timid in the night
Froze to the lion's roar;
A bullfrog croaked;
Returning from his reverie
He heard the crickets sing;

His last church was best,
Wattle, brick and thatch
And constant burning light
That bound him,
To his tabernacle.
Trapped,
He flicked another bottle cap
And thought of home,
From primrose bank
To curlew's call;
The family long gone
That nailed his soul in innocence
On the altar
Of this martyrdom.

He was Columbanus
Bound to Bobbio,
Aiden to Lindisfarne,
And Colmcille
His royal back to home
With Celtic spirit unsubdued,
Unrelenting.

His mind traversed the map,
The churches there, were
Beacons in his wilderness.
It was he who brought the light,
Forgotten now by those who sent
And those he served;
Amid the fragrant bougainvillaea
Bilharzia and baobab
He slept a bitter sleep
Beneath the mango leaves.

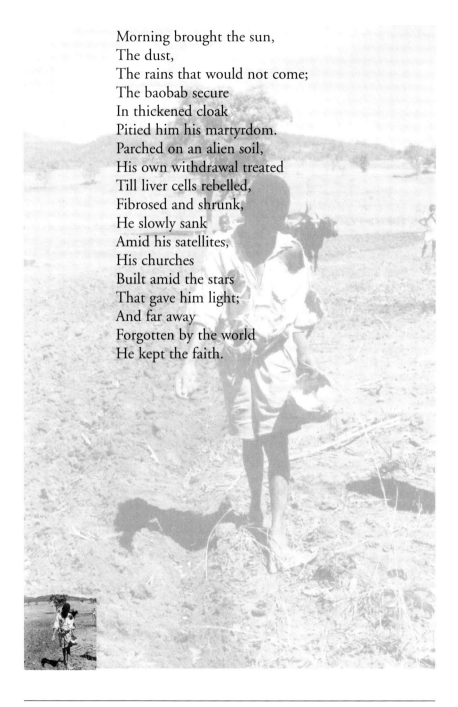

Morning brought the sun,
The dust,
The rains that would not come;
The baobab secure
In thickened cloak
Pitied him his martyrdom.
Parched on an alien soil,
His own withdrawal treated
Till liver cells rebelled,
Fibrosed and shrunk,
He slowly sank
Amid his satellites,
His churches
Built amid the stars
That gave him light;
And far away
Forgotten by the world
He kept the faith.

Clarendon Street

Incense quiet
Asylum,
Ora pro Nobis;
Silent island oasis
In a busy metropolis.

Grafton Street a throb
of drums
and rhythm strings,
of busy push
and Eros call
Perfumed,
Passing
Beautiful.

Inside
Serene faces
Contemplate a mystery,
Their love
That chose the better part
That would not be taken away.
Ora pro Nobis.

Faith

What am I ?
A congregation of ions
Protons, neutrons, electrons
Covalent possibilities,
Consenting atoms
In a twisted helix
Of X and Y
Exchanging chromosomes
In a tingle of existence.

And what is death ?
The edge of nothing,
The bottomless abyss
Where blackness begins

Can I conceive
Of what does not exist ?

Prayer is the mantra
Of repeated reassurances,
Strength for the uncertainty
Of the lonely night
Till meaning seeps through.
Where is Yahweh?
Does anybody listen?

With faith
The mantra
Yields its meanings;
Faith makes God exist
Implying Hope
And demanding Charity.

The God I could not prove,
Nor wanted to,
Is in the heart,
The mind follows after.

Does the mind tell us
Who to love,
Or where, or when or how ?
Does the mind sense
The freshness of the morning,
The bridal spray of spring,
The apple green
In the apple pink of evening ?
Does it see
The beauty in the waterfall
Where the rainbows shelter
Shimmers of the sun?

Does the mind tell us
Right from wrong ?
Or does it merely follow,
Appraising and approving
What we know,
Torturing us for proof.

Persevere,
For what we can conceive
Exists,
Though words constrain,
Though cultures change,
They add harmony
To belief.

Chrism

By Flatford Mill
By Dedham Vale
The Boat Dock empty stands,
Another willow
Bends the gale
To Constable's commands.

By Flatford Mill
The tourists trail
By oar and oar o'er water,
The Hay Wain dips
A passing rail
Its light remains thereafter.

By Waterloo
A train came through,
A boy from home departing,
With chrismed hand
And hallowed brow
The boy and man were parting.

A flash of red
A flick of white
A life to art imparted;
An ideal tied
In collared light
To share what heaven guarded.

Is God a Noun?

Why should God a noun be,
A bearded face on Yahweh,
Benign, and kind or vengeful?

Should God not be a verb?
To do, or be creative,
To see in every seed
The fruit in its creation.

Why should God a noun be,
A Brahmin at Kumbh Mela
Beyond the ice-cold Ganges?

Should God not be a verb?
To throw away what passes,
To keep within the soul
What thoughts inspire and hearten.

Why should God a noun be
A monarch, throne or kingdom,
Beyond a gateway guarded?

Should God not be a verb?
To grow, to love, to pardon,
Where sin is to impede
The growth that hope has garnered.

The School Poem

"You're writing a bit of a poem"
He said
"I love a bit of a poem,
We had powerful ones at school long ago;
They're not like that anymore"

"I remember
"The Burial of Sir John Moore"
A powerful bit of a poem;
An ould lad that died fighting somewhere,
When he died
They took him home"

"The poems are not like that anymore…
The Burial of Sir John Moore…
I remembered it once
From end to end…
'Twas a powerful bit of a poem"

Boarding School

I

So small, so small
Against the granite,
History piled
Above your head;
Tears that welled
Prepared for parting,
Filled with words
That were not said.

So small, so small
Against the granite,
Stone facade
In history old;
Without your spark
Of love and warmth
Your cold grey stone's
Forever cold.

II

Small, still small
Against the granite,
Firmness still
Above your head;
Relenting now
Where once we parted,
Seems to say
"Don't go" instead.

The oak and brass
Have lost their hardness,
The lintel leans
From overhead;
"This was your home
That you were part of,
Come back some day
My friend" it said.

The Hearing Aid

Joe was an eccentric genius.

He bought a new racing bicycle when he was the wrong side of seventy —- dropped handlebars, gears, panniers, the lot.

He cycled from the midlands to Dun Laoghaire, got on the boat to Holyhead, and cycled across England, to fulfil an ambition to visit Lincoln Cathedral, and listen to the bells. When I saw him, in his nineties, his hearing had grown muffled with time. He had to sell the bike to help pay for a hearing aid. An expert had called and had sold him the very latest in technology, the best.

Before calling to Joe, our expert had called to do a hearing check on a Mrs. Reynolds, a neighbour, who had answered an ad in the newspaper. His technique was brilliantly clever. Mrs. Reynolds was in her eighties, and was now living away from home. She was the youngest of eight, most of whom were now dead.

"Does your sister like spaghetti" he asked quickly.

"What is he saying" she turned to me and asked sensibly.

"See! She needs a hearing aid…. she needs two hearing aids", our expert said, "try this"

"Now,

Will you have a banana Mrs. Reynolds" he asked gravely.

"No, I don't like bananas" she answered firmly to this ridiculous request.

"See there! —- Did you notice that improvement" he cried triumphantly.

She got the hearing aid.

Spaghetti how are you! They never had spaghetti in that house, just potatoes and boxty like everyone else.

I was once called to see Joe, late at night, when everyone was sleeping and the world was still. There are a few standard questions

I always like to ask, which yield valuable information, like breath-lessness on lying flat, as a marker for heart failure.

"Do you ever get breathless in bed at night" I asked.

"What"? He said loudly.

"Do you ever get breathless in bed at night?" I half shouted.

"Oh no", he shouted back, "I always get breakfast when I get up in the morning".

When I called to see Joe during a cold spell that winter, he was crouched in front of an open hearth trying to keep warm. A small log spluttered in the big grate, unable to come to life, to cross that critical point between ignition and extinction. A picture of the Sacred Heart was on the wall opposite, with those mournful eyes that follow you about the room. Over the mantelpiece was another picture, that of his prize Hereford bull, with a rosette pinned to his ear. Another rosette was pinned to the corner of the picture frame, faded and gathering dust from years of exposure.

There on the mantelpiece I spotted the hearing aid, still in its box.

"Do you not use the hearing aid Joe?" I asked.

"What?" he said.

"Do you not use the hearing aid?" I shouted louder.

"Ah, I do," he said,

"I put it in when I'm going to bed at night"!

Our expert had long since moved on to new pastures, his expertise and subtlety falling on deaf ears.

Happy Christmas

1

Happy Christmas my arse!
On your knees round the floor
In an alcohol haze
As you crawl through the door

2

Happy Christmas my arse!
On your landing-en-suite,
As you pissed down the stairs
Till the banisters seeped
With the turkey half plucked
And she hoped he'd come home,
While she rushed to the store
For the nutmeg and cloves
That would flavour the turkey
And honeydew ham.

3

Happy Christmas at midnight
Embittered and cold,
An assortment of pills
For oblivion stored,
Bulimic the moods
Anorectic and sore
And no one aware
Of abuses once bore.

4

Happy Christmas with Simon,
Any refuge will do,
Your face is a mask
For a soul black and blue.
The judge in his chamber,
His orders ignored,
There is soup and a manger
And Bethlehem's cold.

5

Happy Christmas alone
Where Penates call home,
A man thumbed a page
With Theophilus Moore,
The moon in its phases
Its high tides and lows
And almanac fairs full
Of horses and stores,
He scanned the predictions
And felt his bones jar,
Thanked God for His goodness
For Cancer his star.

6

"Happy Christmas my darling
You were left there alone
On a coarsened hair mattress
To expire on your own,
With your thoughts widely scattered
On an Alzheimer's rack,
In a chorus of Christmas
The Cheyne-Stoking stopped;

Happy Christmas, from heaven
With God on His throne,
I'm waiting here darling
To welcome you home".

Happy Christmas !

The Millennium

The year,
The century,
The millennium,
Wheezed to its end.

From a flu-bed he watched
Eruptions light the night skies;
Pin-pricks of excitement.
"Imagine" he said "Imagine"
"The song of the millennium!
Did you ever read the words?
The National Anthem of Nihilism!
No heaven, no hell" he whispered
"Nihilism"

"They remember the winners
Do you know who was voted
Musical Genius of the Millennium?
McCartney and Lennon
Joint first,
And Mozart was second!
I'm sure George
In his hospital bed,
Stabbed,
As the millennium
Breathes to a close
Is embarrassed."

The sun
Slipped behind the waves
Beyond The Bull,
The Cow, The Calf
Off Dursey Head;
And when the backward counting clock
Reached naught,
Time just pushed
Through man's barricades.

After The Explosion

We are the lucky ones
We have survived
Deaf and maimed and blind,
We wait in hospital queues,
We are the lucky ones.

We are the lucky ones
Muffled ear drums ruptured,
Silently we wait
Strangers to Beethoven,
Or our own child's cry;
We are the lucky ones,
We have survived.

Dawn breaks
Where daylight never comes,
We recognise the sun
By the warmth
On our skin,
We are the lucky ones.

Others wept
Windswept with their loss,
Salt shed on stone,
But we, the lucky ones
Hold on to life's remnants,
Forever changed
In a hospital queue.

Waking

We talked
And we laughed a bit,
We spent the night with you;
The last you spent
At home with us,
Alone, we spent with you.

You did not mind
Our laughing there,
Your face, your soul restrained,
In silent prompt
To mortal man
In our own lives constrained.

The leaves were crunched
As each one passed,
The autumn gently sighed,
It whispered to the gnarled oak
That sheds each year
With pride.

The Empty Room

The house is quiet now
Since you went away;
The last in the line is gone
Stretching back to infinity
And forth again, in uncertainty.

I walked the empty room
Reproached by silence;
Come back, come back
And toss it with your laugh again
And I will hold my peace.

Miscarriage

I wrote a poem for you today,
It should have been your birthday,
And standing by the window pane
Between potato peels
It came to me
A poem-prayer for your birthday.

I wrote a prayer for you today
Because it was your birthday,
I shared your name,
You came to me,
We prayed between potato peels
Because it was your birthday.

Unplanned

I saw her running
Towards the gate,
Her hand clutched
A menagerie of cowslips,
Crushed higgedly piggedly
In her excitement.

Another day,
She came
A child still
With a vial
To confirm
That she found love,
Though unprepared.
No words exchanged
Except a date
And reassurances.

She left to face the world
With fear and apprehension,
A child with hope
Clutching a handful of cowslips.

Table Talk

Wild duck and pigeon
A duet in red wine and beetroot.
Venison in juniper,
Vacuum packed.

The swallows came today,
Rushed through
Half-opened doors
Twittering excitements out of Africa;
A slave-ship
Tramped the Benin coast
Cramped with children
For the gold-mines,
Love charms and baubles
From Angola.

An April cherry
Avenue sedated
Weighted,
Held its breath,
Ready to explode.
At thirteen he was exhumed,
An itinerant scholar.
Our classes could have crossed.

I went through Lettermullen once
Letterfrack and Carraun,
Heather and larksong,
Salt spray invigorating
The first holiday of a cyclist,
Oblivious
To grey walls and roofs
And unrelenting hiding places,
To eneuritic smells
Pungent with fear,
Unknown until exhumed,
A thirteen year old.

A small girl
With no one's name
Broke ranks one day
In golden hair
To show affection;
Had seen her curls shaved
And shamed again
To re-establish discipline.
Exhumed, she stood
With other ghosts;
Was this our Isle of carers
And intransigent scholars?

The swallows came today
To find their beam,
Their gable end,
Their corbelled corner still the same,
Their world unchanged;
Over sheep silent fields
And cloven pyres of Cumbria,
Over Windermere
And Cooley's wild goat cull,
Over venison and juniper.

We discussed him,
Discussed her,
Discussed it
Over red wine and wild duck.

The Anaesthetic

They gave me a gown with no back
To wear, with my indignity:

Nicholas Ingram had his legs shaved too.
He went to the chair
In Georgia today.
His mother prayed in vain.
There would be no protest here
Except from the Bible folk
Who quoted scripture
Justifyingly
To God's embarrassment.

What if I should not return,
Or sleep for twenty years?
Rip Van Winkle on his monitor.
The children would to strangers grow.
The golfers teed and drove
And walked polite fairways
Beyond the window pane.

The trolley came
And by an alcove stayed,
Where shrouds of equalising green
With gowned eyes were watching.
This was complete surrender.
"A nice day" they said,
Where the arc lights burned overhead,
And far away the whins
Would waste their light
On a hillside of April.
The arc light grew unsteady
And disintegrated.

The pain came seeping back.
"Wake up, wake up"
This pain would be forgiven;
My mind was still intact.
Through departing anaesthesia
The watching eyes were there,
The gowns still green
To prove that I was here.

Had I gone;
Who would have noticed?
The radio spoke the news,
Amid the grapes
And canulas
And water bottles.
There was cruelty on a cattle boat
To Tunisia;
A Spanish boat arrested
Had too much monkfish;
There would have been no place
For me today;
Nicholas Ingram died in Georgia.
A mother wailed
And all was forgotten.

A Wild Primrose

I plucked for you a primrose
Beneath an April snow
That clinging to the blackthorn
Conceived the bitter sloe.

I plucked for you the primrose
That faithful to the sun
Would follow it from year to year,
From dawn till dew drops come.

I plucked for you a primrose,
To fold within your book
A prayer into the silent page
If ever you should look.

I plucked another primrose
To keep within my heart,
Where side by side they grew awhile,
So close, yet so apart.

The Handshake.

We were hopeless underdogs in Croke Park that day. Yet, Offaly hurling had been good to us. We had a magic summer, the year before still fresh in our memories, the early final-whistle during that fight back, the exasperation. We all knew that it was early. The more incensed tore down the aisles of the New Cusack Stand towards the pitch. We stood and watched, for a few moments caught between indignation and decorum.

Ah, what the heck! This would be the only chance to set foot on Croke Park. Down we went, excitement now mellowing our disappointment. A guard took off after one invader, a slip of a girl who squealed as she turned like a hare. The guard lost his cap. This was our chance. He was hopelessly outnumbered. We invaded, sat down peacefully on the hallowed turf, took photographs for the family album, and congratulated ourselves. We congratulated ourselves again when we won a reprieve with a replay in Thurles.

Thurles was electrifying. Blue and gold waving, undulating like a hill field of ripening oats, interspersed with islands of green, white and gold.

"Come on The Banner…"

"Ua Fhaile, Ua Fhaile, Ua Fhaile…"

Joe Dooley swivelling at the corner flag, Johnny Dooley stepping into space where none seemed to exist.

Next year it was Cork in Croke Park again.

The game swung to and fro. John Troy was penalised for picking the ball!!

No way !! No way !!

Anyone else yes, but not John Troy. He was a wizard. The ball just sprang up on his stick. We had seen him do that trick so often before.

In front of me a young man jumped to his feet, eyes blazing, neck vessels straining.

"You're a bastardanarsole ref" he roared out to the blackclad figure, obliviously tootling away on his whistle, "A BASS tardanarsole".

He turned right around, and pleaded with me earnestly…

"Is'int he, Is'int he a…

"He is, he is… I agreed emphatically, cutting across his eloquence, though not knowing what that anatomical absurdity meant, but it seemed apt at the time.

We lost that day.

It was hard to say well done —when it should have been a draw.

But today we had no chance.

Out of loyalty, we were there again, for the last time, out of appreciation for so much entertainment, for so much skill. We would not forsake them now. Cork were everywhere. We were outnumbered six to one - red and white, white and red - a host of international flags red and white too - the sickle, the maple leaf, the rising sun —-

But the script was being changed; the annihilation was not taking place.

No, as the game swung to and fro, Offaly were still there, the Whelehans, Johnny Pilkington, the Dooleys.

They're going to do it! They're going to do it!!

Damn it! there's only ten minutes left, and they're going to do it.

We stood at the final whistle, a row clapping and cheering our heroes home. Why did we ever have a doubt when they did not doubt themselves?

The Cork supporters that day were the most gracious that I ever saw. We were surrounded by them, and yet they reached out the hand —-"fair play to you boy",

"well done"—-"I hope you go all the way now"

We stood facing down towards the field.

A small boy in white and red climbed the steps plodding slowly towards us, part of a disappointed exodus. As he came level with our row he stopped. He was twelve, maybe thirteen. He did not speak. His eyes were welled with tears. He swallowed hard the lump that was in his throat.

He reached across in front of me to where another boy, aged thirteen, in green and white and gold was still clapping. He reached out his hand. Taken by surprise the other boy stopped clapping. They clasped hands, their eyes met. Not a word was spoken.

He swallowed hard and let go again.

I watched him climb slowly up the steps to the exit, following the adults home, his poor heart breaking. Just over an hour before he was only one game away from the Liam McCarthy Cup, and now he was a whole year away, with Tipperary, Clare, Limerick and Waterford in between.

There were many sporting moments that day, that year.

But none could match those few seconds, that instant, when a small boy in red and white, and a heart near breaking, stopped and reached out a hand to a stranger to say

"Well done".

Spring
Casebook

1. *Forgetful*

I'm getting kind of forgetful.
If I could forget everything
I'd be right.
They keep calling me back
But it's a different person
In the outpatients every time.
When they do that
I mustn't be worth cobbling up.
Something will have to happen soon.
I'm long enough in the way.
I can remember what happened
Before I went to school,
But not yesterday.

The heart is all right,
It went a long time too
Between the hoppin' and trottin'.
As ould Johnnie Molloy said
When he got the pension,
I suppose it's the beginning of the end.
No jumping or stopping
Or starting of late
With the heart,
But it's a bit waddly still.

Poor Charlie is not well either,
The man that cuts the timber.
A big strong man one time.
Poor Charlie is not well.

2. Expectations

Daffodils, high on a garden ditch;
Drills moulded lovingly
For spring's incubation.
Charcoal lambs soften
The hash edge of April.
An early dandelion
Folded its petals into evening.

The sharp reminder
Of the Bingo bus
Called. Would she go
Or would she stay?
Maybe if she won
She could give it all away
To ease his pain.
He felt a twinge,
A little bloated now
He did not expect to see
The drills grow.
If only something might work.
He hoped
But could not say.

3.   Out of Reach

A water nymph
Stood in the garden,
Brass naked in the bushes,
Pointing upwards.
The cough was troublesome.
If only he had the energy
To walk around the garden again.
Maybe the new treatment
Would help do that,
To walk around the garden again.
The cigarettes were by the phone.
He stayed in touch
With the outside world,
A world he strode
Less than a year before.
He could not keep his appointment
Because he was away,
In Africa…
America…
If only then…
If only now…
But then, the garden was too far,
Beyond his bathroom reach.
Breathless, he went inside.

4. *The Floodgates*

On previous visits
She would not wait,
Her symptoms a mystery.
Today the floodgates burst.
By accident she heard a story
That could have been her own.
Once she called, and there was no one here.
This was the only place she could call.

On the way home
She saw him
Standing by the traffic lights.
It took all her strength
Not to drive at him,
To kill him,
To make him suffer.
How could she tell anyone
What made her worthless?
And it had happened twice.

But now the floodgates burst,
When she heard another's story
That could have been hers.
Maybe, maybe it would improve from here.

5. *The Novena*

She felt "wake" at the novena.
It was the only place she would go now.
I've terrible trouble with "the pulps" she said.
Someone had called the growth
A euphemistic polyp.
The men were busy with the spring.
A stricture can cause a blockage I explained.
I know about the structure she said
Everyone busy in denial,
The denial of hope deferred,
Hope with its protection.

How do they always have
A new bar of soap,
Cussons labelled,
The kettle always on the boil?
The children are all at home now,
They keep the place alive.
The only place I go now
Is the novena,
But God, I'd hate "the bug".

6. *The Rash*

Her medication was stopped,
There was no point in continuing,
And she didn't feel as good.
She sent for detergent to clean the bath,
But they sent Ammonium Sulphate
By mistake.
It was for removing moss from the lawn.
Her husband used the bath
And got a rash.
He was afraid to get it checked.
He was worried about the rash.
I suppose I can tell him
That he won't come to any harm
And that moss won't grow on him
This summer anyway!

7. Gout

Is it Gout, she said, Gout!
That's from too high a feedin',
And he laughed across his walking frame.
I liked that nurse in the hospital.
I'll get a chair, she said
And here she came
With a wheelchair
And gave me the grandest jaunt
I ever got.
Too high a feedin' he laughed.
The nurse would be back tomorrow
To give him his injection,
And meals on wheels every Thursday.
I was throwing out a few crumbs
To the birds,
They might as well be picking at them
As any thing else.
The weather isn't too hard
On them yet.
You know,
I wouldn't mind leading my life
All over again,
And I wouldn't change a thing!

Autumn
Casebook

1. *The Widow's Mite*

"I was waiting here all week," she said
"I knew you'd come sometime.
It's so late; you could have left it
Till tomorrow.
I think the diabetes is OK,
My book is there....
Is four point four all right?
The first time you called I had the coma,
And, the towel is there
By the basin.

Do you see the round tin
In the corner?
I saved a pot of damson jam
For you,
And mind yourself on the road;
You could have left it
Till tomorrow".

2. *Anniversary*

It's anniversary time again
That bitter sweet remembering time of year,
When you come back to me.

"We were too close", they said.
But what was I to do?
Five years have given way since then,

Five years
With summer's growth unshared,
Each day of which

I shared with you.

3. *Saying Hello*

He was neither
Aggressive nor disruptive.
He had two bottles,
One for the day
And one to help him sleep.
When "meals on wheels" arrived
It was his last visit of the day,
And what was he to do then?
If he went to the hospital
They would try to change him,
And "give out",
He said,
And he would only fight
With everyone.

He needed two bottles,
One to help him eat
And one to sleep.
It was Friday,
His day for shaving
And tidying up,
And when he died
He would be content,
And that would be
The end
Of him.

4. *The High Court*

Contiguous circles
Beneath Gandon's dome,
Perpetual motion;

An atom peels off
In wig and gown,
Horse-trading
To find another circle;

Plaintiff, defendant,
Expert witness;
All calm exteriors,
Duck-serene on the water
Feet paddling furiously underneath;
Palpitations, tachycardia,
Perspiration, panic
Settled with a sigh.

The Tipstaff crossed the floor;
The waters parted
As in Exodus.
The circles disintegrate,
Evaporate
In relief
And in disappointment.

5. Controlling the Waves

I am a barque
Light and airy,
Tossed on life's waves
On a sea in turmoil.

Sometimes afraid
I gasp for breath
In the crash of crest
And trough surrender.

Sometimes I float;
I soak the sun, the salt,
The tangled seaweed,
And glimpse the coral gems of ages.

Can I relax
To trust the ebb and flow,
That takes me to the shore,

Or striving with the moon
Do I control the waves?

6. *November*

I hate November,
I hate November with
Its dark down days;
I lie awake and wait
At night
And when the lights turn in
I hate having worried.
And now that he is safe at home
I say "I'll never do that again".

When the flowers start to bud
I lift,
I lift with the springtime
But I hate November.
I'm in my dark cloud now
And I can't get out.
It has closed in on me!
I hate November.

7. Unequal Roads

Her smile reached out
Into the future,
Innocent
With anticipation.
"Would I ring
The only number on her cell phone
And explain
His fractured rib,
His pain,
His pneumothorax.
Then they would believe"

She left,
Echoing appreciation.
The phone was answered,
The voice, mature, strong,
Restrained.
"Yes," he said
"He would tell the prison doctor"

Limericks
&
Mini-Sagas

Limericks

Though Limericks can sometimes be rude
The contents should never be crude,
Where beneath all the chaff
You can winnow a laugh
With the kernel of sense that ensued.

The Mini-saga

A mini-saga is a short story
Of exactly fifty words.
It has a beginning, a middle and an end.
It is a structured discipline
But with a weakness;
You tend to count the words instead
Of concentrating on the content.
If this was one, are you tempted to count?

Truthfully?

The Weight Watcher

A weight watcher using his head
Told his class they had pounds they should shed.
So reducing the size
Of their avoirdupois
He increased his pounds sterling instead.

Driving to Exercise

Up and down, up and down,
They stepped, aerobically,
Rhythmically.
Her grandfather whistled behind the plough
And strode after the horse harrow.
He would have been proud of her success.
The car park behind the gymnasium
Was always full.
He had often walked that road,
Where cars queued
For exercise.

The Academic

A doctor was so erudite
That he published to show he was bright,
Then to add to his score
Published ten papers more
To prove that his first wasn't right

The Gastroscopy

The Consultant was adamant.
"Your symptomology suggests
A gastro-oesophageal reflux,
The probable aetiology of which
Is the Heliobacter organism.
We will admit you for urgent gastroscopy
And investigative biopsy"

"They are taking me into hospital tomorrow"
He said when he got home
"They want me to ate a camera".

The Consultant

A consultant asked to diagnose
Said "your health is quite good I suppose,
But I'll see you twice more
To be sure, to be sure,
Before your account I can close".

Reassurance

"Well, how's the heart?" he asked apprehensively,
Palms moist with anticipation.
His father had trouble with the heart
About his age, and his father before him.
"How is it?" he ventured again.
The doctor discarded the stethoscope.
"It will do" he said,
"It will do
For going around the house".

The Politician

A man of political bent
In circumlocutions gave vent.
With each passing word
He grew more absurd,
And concealed what he said that he meant.

The Butterflies

"I know exactly how to beautify our village"
The secretary of the Tidy Towns committee announced.
"We will plant trees and shrubs
So that the birds will sing,
And the butterflies will be happy".
The next day she bought the best insecticide
To save her cabbage
From those ugly caterpillars.

The Pathologist

A doctor once frightened to bits
That a patient might sue him with writs,
Said his only recourse
The pathology course!
Now a ghost has him scared of his wits

Disappointment

"They are taking me into hospital tomorrow,
To do an autopsy", he announced, pleased.
He had waited a long time for his appointment,
But an autopsy!
All he had was an itch!
"Could it ever be a biopsy?" I ventured.
"Well, something like that" he said,
His confidence now shattered!

The Barrister

A barrister curled and gowned,
Had a smile up his sleeve when he frowned;
With illogical grace
He would lose every case
Which he won when the bills were sent round.

The Explosion

The bishop visited the hospital
After the explosion. He wore purple.
The patients were happy, their morale boosted.
The colonel, braids and epaulets,
Visited the soldier,
Whose ulnar nerve was shattered,
His hand forever useless.
The eagle on his forearm, his tattoo
Was disfigured.

He was broken-hearted over the eagle.

The Dance

In Limerick their dance is "the walls"
And the "siege" out in Ennis enthrals.
But students I find
Are now more inclined
To talk about Debutantes Balls.

Changing Cultures

It was the end of an era.
He was going away to school.
The culture might be different.
"Don't ever forget the language"
He was told apprehensively.

"I bet you don't know the Irish for cricket"
He called, on his first weekend home,
Aiming his bat towards a setting sun.

The Scribe

A doctor his fortune to seek
Wrote verse to acclaiming critique,
But his patients averred
His prescriptions preferred
So he's stuck with his Chaucer's Phisik

The Split Infinitive

The computer had fifty thousand bytes,
And fifty million characters.
It had an encyclopaedia, a thesaurus and a dictionary.
It had a spellcheck,
Wordcheck, colons, semicolons,
Hyphens and parentheses.
It had a screen to automatically retrieve information.
It showed us how
To almost reach infinity,
And to proudly split infinitives.

Spleen,
Scalpel
&
Secateurs

Creative Writing

Words are dried flowers
Skillfully arranged
In baskets
Of inaccessability,
Admired
By critics
With words
That are dried flowers.

Flowers are words
That erupt each spring,
Snowdrop petals and crocus,
Primula and daffodil
And bluebell
Wild on a mountain ledge
Leading to
Chrysanthemums for Christmas,
Arranged in a poem
Renewed each year
In innocence.

Casualty Officer

When icon spoke of icon in vignette
And Poet's pen reviewed in paid bequest,
When giant published giant to excess,
What could we do but bow, in feigned aspect.

When titan spoke of titan in egress
With iambs rolled from pedestal's regret,
When feet of fashion followed trends now set,
What could we do but feign and bow express.

Can we not feel with love of equal depth?
Have we not seen our nights and loves upset
As late we strain to save from passion's debt
The famed reduced to fameless self neglect.

The great can pen their failures to success,
The swan, unpenned, will bow his shared respect.

Celebrity

They come to life
Lizard like
In the arc lights.
The stage revolves,
The cameras turn,
And in a blink
The screen becomes alive,
The papers breathe vitality.

Transmuted there
They tell us
How to live, to love,
To make success
Of our
Apparent commonplace.

Envious,
We dream
Their dreams,
Of alchemy,
Glitter dripping,
Articulate,
Artifice.

The arc lights fade,
The cameras turn away,
The cold of loneliness pervades,
And in a blink
They shrink
Lizard like again
On forgotten stones
To wait the public dawning
Of their new day.

Le Tour

Joe, Joe, Say it's not true Joe;
You that climbed the Tourmalet,
Luz Ardiden from Gave de Pau,
Say it's not true Joe.

I stood by the cross in Blessington
To watch the Tour go past,
Where firemen scoured for hours
Their highway clean to nowhere ———
To everywhere —-
To Glendalough, by Kevin's glen,
Past *Tonlegee*, arse to the wind,
Salt drip on gripping bars,
Through Analecka bridge;
Those diabolic climbs,
Those anabolic lows,
Say it's not true Joe.

I saw a monument to Tom today,
A limestone on Ventaux,
The cameras swoop there once a year
To take our hero home.
Amphetamines they gave you Tom,
Your mind could not control;
Your dreams of Alpine glory stole,
Transmuted there in stone.

I stood by the cross in Blessington
And watched my innocence go past;
Hippocratic oaths forsworn
Parading to the Alps,
Pawns to the podium
On a cordoned road of West Wicklow;
Sub iugum went the slaves to Rome
Beneath their masters' glow.
The oxygen was scarce today
Without the EPO,
Two bikelengths of haematocrit
Would make a difference Joe.

I saw a beautiful woman once,
Flo first to the line,
Less androgenic then,
And men in wonder
Why their manliness had shrunk.

Joe, Joe, Say it's not true,
But innocent faces I saw there too.

The Good Samaritan

The Good Samaritan turned his head
And looked the other way,
He didn't see his brother fall
Or hear what he might say.
I passed this way one day before
Pray pardon if I'm rude,
I tried to treat a poor man's wounds,
"The hoor" he said "he sued".

I gave him oil, I gave him wine,
The priest passed by he sobbed,
"No point in stopping here" said he,
"That man's already robbed".
I patched him up, I bound his wounds,
I gave him board and food,
I gave him transport on my ass…
When he got home, he sued.

I once had thoughts to cure the world,
To heal the wrongs I saw,
But now I've stopped the curing,
Instead, I'm doing law.
I will not see, I will not hear,
Success has now accrued
Since I have changed to wig and gown
Because somebody sued.

The Traffic Lights

The Councillors were worried
With the traffic in the town,
And discussed about a hundred ways
To get it to slow down,
Till at last there came a motion
With a most ingenious plot
That not only slowed the traffic down
But froze it to the spot.

They would paint out little boxes
Where the road and pathways meet
And would angle them at forty five
Degrees along the street,
With their noses pointing inwards
They would trap you by the snout
As you parked your car half skew-ways
With the tail boards sticking out.

To make the plan successful
They decided with delight
If it wasn't disrespectful
To erect their own red light,
For they figured for the loiterers
They trapped in ways perverse
That the only way back out again
Was rev up in reverse.

The strategy was simple.
When the lights would turn to red,
The cars would all reverse again
And block the road ahead.
And drivers coming inwards
With politeness that was new
Would nod at empty spaces
As across the road they'd slew.

The plan was so effective
That one morning on the beat
A guard gave parking tickets
In the middle of the street.
And a man going home at dinner time
Thought "what am I to do"?
Took out his Simplex crossword
And filled in every clue.

A load of pigs was squealing
With delight they had perceived
They were stuck so long in traffic
That they thought they were reprieved.
And a van half full of figrolls
Was stuck across the square
As the man now doing crosswords
Was starting his Crosaire.

A lorry at the supermarket
Started to unload
Ten thousand tissues softly
In rolls across the road.
And a Publican caused bottle necks
With traffic at its peak,
Just muttered to his flagons
They'll remember "Jacobs Creek".

There were peas and beans and cornflakes
And Milky Moos and Mars,
And cat food packed on pallets
And salad cream in jars.
The lights were green, the traffic stuck
In pickups and in vans
'Twas a woman was reversing
But a man that drew the plans.

The Vet, the Priest, the Doctor,
Had never seen the like
If they heard the call was urgent
They'd be better oil the bike,
The Fire Brigade was screaming
With hoses to wash down
The blatant case reported
Of arson round the town.

And still from darkness light can come
Our troubles to devour
The only hold up in the town
Is Gridlock for an hour.

The Wind off the Willows

"We're safe, We're safe" the Badger cried
Across an evening ditch,
The Fox jumped up behind Knockirr,
His nose began to twitch.
"We're safe", cried out the Badger,
"We're vectors on a shelf,
Diseases man thought once we spread
He said he'll try himself".

"Hurrah for Homo Ophalus
Who issued this decree
With loads of something scrofulous
He sent us out for free".
The Rat sat in a water-cut
As lorries trundled by;
He knew about the spirochete
But turned a jaundiced eye.

His thoughts were Epicurean
For bellywaste and spleen,
His taste buds growing succulent
His liver turning green.
The wind stirred in the willows
And disturbed them where they grew,
There was something rich fermenting
And they knew which way it blew.

The Badger cried out "Ratty"
As they watched the evening fall,
"We'll have to call our friend the Toad
Who lives down at Toad Hall".

Belly Waste

The cattle are slaughtered,
The pigs are all slain,
We'll shoulder the carcass
And pocket the gain;
But what will we do
With intestines and tails?
We'll find a location
And dump the entrails,
We'll find a location
And dump the entrails.

There's a hill outside Carbury
Where the Boyne River flows,
And the salmon of knowledge
Told Finn all he knows;
It's a perfect location
Without proper roads,
We'll send the Artics out
To dump a few loads,
We'll send the Artics out
To dump a few loads.

There's no need to worry
About any disease,
We've Brucella Marcella
Right up to our knees,
It's a perfect location
A long way from home,
And in the brown envelope
Only a poem,
And in the brown envelope
Only a poem.

Remember Kilcock
With the blue and white flag,
Where the hunter gave chase
To the buck and the stag,
We don't want the entrails
They're not in good taste
So keep all your offal
And your belly waste,
So keep all your offal
And your belly waste.

The Celtic Tiger

(with apologies to O'Leary)

The Celtic Tiger's nearly gone,
He's on a trolley bed in Naas.
They'll want the plug when he moves on
There's not a bed about the place.

The Celtic Tiger's nearly gone
And feeble now his mighty roar,
His pulse is weak, his face is wan
He's on a drip behind the door.

The Celtic Tiger's nearly gone
His caring touch we'll feel no more
For once he nursed, and taught the world
And brought his faith from shore to shore.

The Celtic Tiger's nearly gone,
The "Third World" owes us one debt more,
We need their workers, pay them well
With buttons from our secret store.

The Celtic Tiger's almost done
The Nasdaq has him mauled and gored,
Asylum seekers lined outside
To re-import what once we owned.

Glossary

Revisiting -   **Page 2**

Sheugh -   *drinking pool*

Forninst us -   *opposite us*

Haeved -   *to lead a trump card*

Drait -   *non trump card*

Scuaibín -   *the last game of the night where everyone places their stake in a pool for the winner, as distinct from paying at the end of each game which is usual.*
(It could also mean a game of cards at a fair where the owner of the cards joins in without putting down a stake)

White Martyrdom - Page 18

Bilharzia -   *a water borne infection that penetrates the skin and affects the liver.*

Bougainvillea and Baobab -
    flowering plant and tropical tree that coexists where Bilharzia is endemic

Dik-Dik -   *Small antelope*

Yahweh -   *the personal name of the God of the Israelites, meaning "He Brings into Existence whatever Exists"*

Happy Christmas - Page 30

Penates -   *the household gods*

Cheyne-Stoking -
    terminal breathing named after Dublin physicians John Cheyne and William Stokes

Table Talk - Page 40

Letterfrack -   *one of the Irish correction schools*

eneuretic -   *eneuresis is bedwetting*

A Wild Primrose - Page 45

April Snow -   *Seamus Ennis has composed a piece of music called April Snow, which describes the April blossom on the blackthorn.*

Le Tour - Page 79

Tonelegee -   *mountain on Wicklow Gap road to Glendalough. Literal meaning of the name is back to the wind, tón le ghaoth.*

Ventaux -   *landmark climb of the Tour de France where Tom Simpson died in the Alps.*

Sub Iugum -   *under the yoke. Soldiers conquered by the Roman armies were made to pass beneath spears fixed into the ground in an arch, as a form of forced submission and hence the word subjugation.*